Papillon Rising

AF623498

Bethany Blount

BookLeaf Publishing

Presentation by *BookLeaf Publishing*

Web: www.bookleafpub.com

E-mail: info@bookleafpub.com

ISBN: 9789357211628

First edition 2023

DEDICATION

To the advocates, survivors, and partners I encountered at Bridges Domestic Violence Shelter--

I cannot thank you enough for the life-giving support. This book has been manifested by you because of the love and faith you had in me before I could ever believe in it myself.

ACKNOWLEDGEMENT

Innumerable thanks to the BookLeaf Editors, without whom this book would not have been published.

PREFACE

I hesitated to write this book for so long. Much of this book was written with a shaky hand and a lot of prayers for courage. I am blessed to have a long line of other women who have published similar works before me, and I am grateful for their leadership and inspiration.

I only began writing this book when I was sure that I could write it as an encouragement, not a manifesto of anger.

I wanted it to begin at the ending of my relationship with an abusive partner and to chronicle my life afterwards. On my healing journey, I did have to look back to the past to move forwards, but I decided that I want this book to communicate that your life will not stop or end after escaping domestic/dating violence. With time, you will discover that you are now a completely different person, and have a long life and a lot of joy still left ahead of you.

This was my experience--I went into shelter for several months, and was then under the protective umbrella of the shelter for another year. During this transitional period, I kept to myself, relearning how to be emotionally healthy and to trust my own thoughts and feelings. If we are speaking in "papillon"/butterfly terms, this was my chrysalis period, where I had to dissolve what was uncomfortable and no longer suited me to become something new.

For the past several months, I feel that I've emerged from my chrysalis, but I've been clinging to it, drying my wings. This book represents my first flight-- my re-emergence back into the world, and telling the truth of what I've experienced in a semi-public setting for the first time.

Clarity at the Lake

The last day I was with him,
We went to the lake
To walk and take pictures
Of the wildlife.

He had asked me
To carry his camera bag
And I had agreed.

He insisted on keeping it unzipped
So he could get to his
Zoom lenses.
That worried me,
But I didn't say no—
No, I couldn't say no.
It wasn't worth the fire
And brimstone
To say it.

After walking for 20 minutes,
I forgot to worry about the lid,
The way I was standing,
And walking correctly to make sure
That the unsecured lenses
Wouldn't shatter if I tripped.

I forgot to worry--and enjoyed a moment.
I saw a puppy on the paved road,
The tiniest scruffiest teacup Yorkie
Known to man, with a pink bow
And a pink rhinestone leash.
She ran up to me, tail nub wiggling,
Fur sticking out like a cotton ball
And I reached down to pet her and

"BE CAREFUL!"
I froze—muscles stiff—invisible bars slammed
Back down around my body
"YOU'RE GOING TO BREAK IT!"
I shook as I straightened up
"THOSE ARE EXPENSIVE!"
I felt so small and stupid
"I DON'T CARE IF THERE IS A PUPPY"

The young girl holding the leash looked at me.
She was frightened
And confused
And a little sad
Eyes questioning why he was talking to me this way.
Our eyes met
And I dropped mine back to the dirt.

"IF YOU CAN'T HOLD IT OPEN THEN DON'T HOLD IT AT ALL."

I watched her walking away and could feel
That my eyes were dead
Empty
Voids.

My brain shrank back down to the
Dried up kernel of fear
It had been in the months
Before we tried to start over.

I stared as he approached
Behind me,
Reminding me how
“SELFISH” “DISRESPECTFUL”
“INCONSIDERATE”
“IMMATURE” “IRRESPONSIBLE”
“WITHOUT A CARE FOR OTHER’S
PROPERTY”
I was.

He continued,
Endlessly, as
We walked the beautiful lake trail,

Until I verbalized my agreement
With his assessment of my character defects,
Knowing that he wouldn’t stop
Until I did.

We stopped so he could take pictures
Of the lake.
I stared at the trees across the water,
Not thinking.
He jerked me out of my silence
And said,
"Look at the cardinals."
His bright, boyish smile returned,
Basking in the sun of his rightness,
Forgetting how disgusting
I was to him only minutes before.

I looked at my favorite birds.
There was a crimson male
With his brown mate
Sitting on the bare winter branches
In front of us.
I felt numb.

He took out his camera.
The shutter snapped
And I flinched.

"Oh look," he said, his voice dripping with
childish sweetness,
"He's feeding her."
He turned back to me again,
Beaming, exuberant,
Expecting me to tell him,

As I used to,
That he took care of me
In the same way.

I remained silent and still
Like a garden statue
Staring at the birds
Watching him
Out of the corner of my eye.
It had been 5 minutes since
He had stopped berating me.

I watched the male cardinal
Drop down from the branch
And fly back up to land
With a perfectly ripe berry
Next to his wife.
He offered it to her.
She took it and ate, spilling
The seeds and skin
Messily onto the ground.

He waited until she had finished
The first berry, then swooped
Back down to get her another.

Once, she dropped the whole berry
And he swooped to catch it,
Landing back on the branch to

Patiently offer it to her again.

He was seamlessly attentive, dedicated,
And peaceful.
She remained on the branch,
Waiting for her love,
Satisfied, tranquil, with her
Wings folded delicately to her sides.

My eyes filled with tears.
Out of the corner of my eye,
My boyfriend turned away in disappointment.
I could feel in my chest
That he was pained from my emotion
As if I had ripped his soul into pieces.
He began shaking his head and muttering
About how overly sensitive I was,
Saying quietly,
“I just wanted to have one good day with you.
Is that too much to ask?”

I didn’t respond.
I didn’t have the energy to pretend anymore.
I looked out again across the lake--
It was clear as glass, reflecting the
Cloudless sky and pine trees on the other side
Reflecting the horizon—
And I wondered

Why a songbird knew
How to treat his mate well, while
A human did not.

Two-Way Call: Me

I am leaving you.
I have told you multiple times
That the way you treat me
Is unacceptable.

I broke up with you
And only got back together with you
Because you promised to change.
You promised to stop being controlling of me,
To allow me to go out for drinks
With my friends from work,
To get the 4 small tattoos I wanted,
To wear the clothes I wanted to.

You promised to stop insulting me,
Telling me that I was promiscuous,
Incapable of change, Without self-control,
Incapable of making good decisions,
Having the intelligence
Of a third grader.

I made promises too that I didn't keep.
I promised to be better at cleaning
And being on time
And budgeting my money.

I didn’t keep those promises
And I’m sorry.

But that doesn’t mean I’m
Deserving of the hate
You force me to swallow.

And you refuse to stop.
I’m so confused—
I thought you loved me.

Why would you ask me to return
The gifts you gave to me?
Or to pay you for them?
No! I’m not doing that.
(I think to myself—That’s so petty,
He obviously doesn’t care about me.)

I think I deserve better.
I think I deserve someone
Who understands that their behavior
Can’t be blamed on my issues.
You seemed to understand that
For a while,
And I thought you loved me.
But it’s obvious that you don’t.

(End call)

Two-Way Call: Him

Why are you leaving me?
I know you told me to stop treating you
In the ways you found unacceptable,
But you…you…

…We broke up
And got back together
Only because you promised to change.
You promised to stop controlling me
By trying to go out for drinks
With your friends from work when I said no,
To not get any tattoos that I didn't approve
To not wear the clothes you wear for attention.

You promised to stop insulting my intelligence
By expecting me to lie and say you're faithful,
Capable of change, self-controlled,
Capable of making good decisions,
And smarter than the average
Third grader.

The real issue is you not keeping your promises:
To not be the lazy, messy,
Tardy, disorganized
Spendthrifting gold-digger

I knew you to be.
Admit you didn't keep them. NOW!

You are nothing
But deserving of bitter truth about who you are.
I've asked you to understand,

And you refuse to.
So, I'll ask you one question:
"Why don't you love me?"

Why wouldn't I ask for you to return
The gifts I stupidly got you?
Or to pay me for them?
No?! That confirms what
I knew all along: that you never
Gave a shit about me.

I deserve better than you.
I deserve to be loved by someone
Who understands that their issues
Are what cause me to act out of character.
You understood that
For a while,
And I thought you loved me.
But it's obvious that you don't.

(End call)

The Quiet Tree

I walked past the trees,
Along the flowered path, and
Into a haven.

My heart pounding loud,
I laid down my bags while the
Inner weight remained.

"Legally homeless,"
Two words: scary, hopeful(?)
"Under protection."

Holding my stuffed bear,
I sit on the bed, hunching…
I breathe but don't cry.

In shelter, I slept and slept,
Repaying a year's sleep-debt.

The Secret Life of Butterflies

In one of my favorite books,
"The Secret Life of Bees,"
A young girl flees abuse
To find the mothering,
Sisterhood,
And hope that she never had before.

In shelter, it was the same.
A group of women:
Advocates, small children,
And a dog or two were all jumbled
Together.

We were always laughing
(when we weren't crying), making jokes
About the ridiculous things our
Exes used to say,
Giggling through our tears.

When we made excuses for
Our abusers,
We reminded each other
That if our friend told us this,
We wouldn't excuse it.

We were all mirror images
Of each other,
Many and the same,
Reflecting endlessly a single girl
Standing in the carnival funhouse,
But viewed from different angles.

When we spoke together we were fierce.

At times,
We may not have brushed our hair
Or teeth
Or showered for days
Or eaten anything but chicken tenders
And ice cream,
But we were still the same people.

We discovered again that we were
Loving, compassionate, caring,
Beautiful, kind, considerate,
And intelligent.
We relearned that we were empathetic,
Helpful, mothers of ourselves, our children,
And each other.

One day, I took my inhaler outside with me
So that conversations with my friends
Who smoked cigarettes wouldn't be interrupted
By my asthmatic cough.

The next day, they saw me coming, we talked,
And as I sat down, they put out their cigarettes
And moved the ash tray six feet away from me.

In shelter,
We knew we were safe, cared for,
And loved.
We were able to rest, grow and awaken
Every day
The same, but different—
Like butterflies unfurling their wings to reveal
The pearlescent color
Decorating their luminous bodies.

What Is A Man?

In recovery, I found myself
Wondering what a man
Should be, what a man is told to be,
And what I should expect
From the men in my life.

I was raised to believe that I
Was inherently lesser as a woman,
Was supposed to take up less space,
Blend into the background,
Keep quiet and don't argue,
Remain submissive,
Cover up those lust-inducing shoulders
And smile,
Smile,
Smile---
No matter what happened to me.

In shelter I decided
That all of that was bullshit.

I worked
At a big-box hardware store
In the Lumber and Garden sections.
The men in the lumber section

Were grandfather figures.

One gave me book recommendations,
Listened to mc talk about how much
I wanted a doglike cat,
And told me that a man who tries to
Control others
Has a void of insecurity inside of himself.

Another always offered me a slice of the pizza
He ordered on Friday nights,
And a third honked the forklift horn each time
He passed my register in greeting.

On the Garden side, I had father figures,
Who told me about their former lives up north,
And there were war veterans
Who encouraged me to breathe
And took over my register
When I thought I saw my ex coming.

And there were guys my age who
Asked me questions
About my interests
When I was chatting with them
While stocking sodas.

I hadn't had anyone take an interest
In my thoughts in a very long time.

I later joined a boxing gym.
I showed up every day there
With my hair in a messy bun
And ratty athletic clothes,
Huffing, puffing, and 60 lbs overweight
From all the emotional eating I did
When I was with my ex.

I expected the guys to look
And sneer a bit at my size.

Instead, one guy offered me his lunch
When he had decided not to eat it.
Every muscled-up guy in that gym
Treated me with respect and kindness.

My abuser, in comparison--
Instead of controlling himself, he controlled
"his women."
Instead of being vulnerable, he shut down
My vulnerability.
Instead of being honest,
He lied and yelled at me for
"being crazy" and "paranoid."

He measured his self-worth
Based on the extent of how absolutely
I adored him, whether I

Disagreed with him in any way,
Or whether I had committed a serious,
Relationship-altering sin such as
Talking too much about
My roommate's cat
Or the books I was into
Or how much fun I was having with my plants.

I saw for the first time how childlike
His tactics were—
He was a grown man
Who mocked my terrified voice and tears
And said during arguments,
"Ha-ha, you said it, I was right,
You can't take it back now!"
In the same voice that a four-year-old uses
To call another kid
A "stinky stupid" on the playground.

I figured my ex out--
And I learned from the other men
That a true man
Respects people as individuals.

A Broken Doll

I stared at the photo card
In front of me.
A dirty plastic baby doll
With one eye stared back at me.

I picked it up.
"This is how I feel,"
I said to my therapist,
hand shaking.

I didn't fully understand why.
I just knew that my body
Felt numb, rubbery,
And that it was for others to use,
Not for me.

One night
When he had too much
To drink,
I leaned against his dining room wall,
Inviting him to come over and kiss me.

He looked at me,
Then broke into a wide smile,
Eyes unfocused.

He lurched towards me,
Still grinning
Like a mako shark,
Eyes black,

And forced me
Against the wall
Upwards,
Slamming his knee into my crotch
Until my feet dangled.
The back of my head hit the wall
My shoulder blades scraped painfully
Against the cheap beige paint
My crotch was pinched against the wall
And hurt from the pressure of his leg.

He didn't say a word,
Just looked at me
Like a predator.
I froze and began ineffectually
Trying to push away from him,
Completely ignoring his gaze,
Staring over his shoulder at
His microwave oven.
I can't remember if I said no.

He backed away and lowered me
To the ground,

Watching me
As I stumbled into
The beanbag chair on the floor.

He didn’t say anything until
I began to cry,
Then rushed to me,
Apologizing and telling me that
It was an accident,
That he just had too much to drink
And lost control for a second
And that I was overreacting
And it was no big deal
And nothing even happened
So we should move on from it.

I cried, “When you did that something
Broke inside of me.”

That was the first time
I felt like the dirty baby doll
Thrown into the dumpster
And discarded.

A Broken Doll, Pt. 2

Months later,
After I had learned that
I couldn't say no to him,
Couldn't stick up for myself in arguments,
And wasn't allowed my separate personhood,

His extra credit lesson was that my body
Was another of his possessions
That he could ask for
Like a candy bar.

If I said no,
It was better to say yes
Because my life's purpose
Was to make him happy.

I told him not to spank me
Because of the fear and pain
Of my childhood spankings
And he found a way to forget
That I said no
And that I didn't like that.

I told him at first that I didn't want to
Be called a whore or a bitch,

That I didn't want to take part
In his fetishes,
That I didn't want him to make
Me touch him under his boxers.
But over time I was molded into
The robot that fit his preferences perfectly
And didn't have her own in her factory settings.

He took parts of my body without asking,
And asked for forgiveness, not permission.
Every time he "just got too excited"
Or said that my reluctance
Made him feel unwanted.

My psyche was still alert enough
And put up enough of a fight to keep
Him from ever taking my virginity
That I was saving for marriage,
And from ever putting himself into my mouth,
But every time I refused,
He would retreat like a sad puppy
Who had been denied a second treat.

For everything else,
He pushed and pushed
And begged and begged
And kept asking
And asking
And asking

Until eventually I was convinced
That I was the one
Saying yes,
Not the sex doll he had created,
Who responded with ten different
Sound effects
When touched in a certain way.

Egg

My home growing up
Was--difficult and complicated.

I was always afraid,
Although I couldn't name
My feeling.
I never spoke up—
I felt I wouldn't
Be heard, or worse, be punished
For speaking.

I retreated into books,
Because I was told
By my family that the outside
World was dangerous
And unsafe, full of people
Who would one day hurt me,
While my home was chaotic.

I was constantly
On alert for when the next missile
Would hit the war zone.
I made my room into my foxhole—
I left my dirty clothes on the floor
And left pens and books there as well

So that if anyone wanted to get at me,
They really had to try.
It hurt to live like that—
I stubbed my toes on my books
And scraped myself with the pens
On the floor,
But once I was on my bed,
No one could get to me.
I sat alone but safe.

Egg, Pt. 2

As a teenager I was taught that image
Was everything,
Especially family image.

I learned that as a girl,
I should do my makeup
So that I would look attractive
For the boys at school.

I was reminded that
If I didn't stop biting my nails,
Slouching,
Keeping my head down,
That no one would notice me--
I wouldn't have friends
And definitely not a boyfriend.

I was told that thinness
And prettiness was the currency
Of success,
And that pretty people
Always had it better in the world.

When I began working as a teenager,
I discovered that I could use my money

To buy the things that the pretty people had.

I had decided that they were the ones
Who were wanted and loved
In this world, not me,
And I devoted too much time to planning
How I would make sure that my image
Matched theirs,
So that I would be loved too.

It was never enough.
The pressure
Of needing to be thin or lose weight,
To get perfect grades,
To do my hair and my makeup every day,
To never make a mistake,
To uphold the family image,
To be the good Christian girl,
Finally got to me.

I had a psychotic break when I was 22.

It took a year of meds
And therapy
But I managed to shed
Most of the negative parts
Of my upbringing
And hatch into the real world.

Larva

When I met my ex,
I was vulnerable.
He was the savior who
I looked to, to help me
Figure out how
To be a person,
To have self-esteem,
To be loved,
And to love others,
And he taught me the beginnings of that,
For a while.

I desperately needed him
To tell me what to think
Because my brain was too broken
At times to think for itself.
Parts of shedding my old self
Were extremely painful—

I found myself crying and sobbing
And hating myself for being unable
To shut up the horrid thoughts,
The voices taunting other people
In my head and encouraging me to
Sneer at them too.

But I refused to.
It took months, but I refused
And finally quieted them down.
I developed my own voice.
I developed the ability to truly love.
I developed my own sense of confidence
And self-esteem.

And that's when all hell broke loose
In my relationship.

Larva, Pt. 2

I was feeling wonderful--
I was developing my own style
And experiencing a delayed
Teenage rebellion that thankfully
Contained itself to my personal style.

I loved my purple lipstick
And my dip dyed hair
And the occasional top
That showed just an inch
Of midriff.
I was so excited to be
Expressing myself
In the world for the first time.

But then,
The doors to the outside world
Slowly started to creak shut.
My ex would say,
"I really don't like lipstick,
Especially the dark stuff"
And wouldn't show me the
Same love
If I insisted on wearing it.

He was jealous of the compliments
I got from random girls I met
About my hair
And my lipstick,
And my outfit.
I was beaming from the inside out
Because I was truly living—
And then he told me that
I was only doing all those things
For the attention of others.

"Why do you need to wear
That shirt? Who are you trying to
Impress?"
--The sunny window to my sense of style
Creaked shut and locked.

"Why do you want any tattoos?
Anybody who gets tattoos only
Gets it for attention, not because
Of the personal meaning…"
--The skylight to sharing my faith and
Encouraging other hurting people
cracked and shattered.

They all locked and shattered one by one
And he began to ask
What happened to the girl
He fell in love with.

Larva, Pt. 3

I lost myself,
Piece by painful piece,
Over a year.
Over that year I spent hundreds
Of hours
On the phone with him,
Trying to convince him that
I was still worthy of loving
And that I loved him.

I was told that disagreeing
With him was stubborn,
Selfish, and being defensive.

I wasn't changing
My trauma-rooted bad habits
Of overspending and messiness
Fast enough for him
And it was embarrassing for him
To be around me when I
Refused to be responsible.

I cried
At least three times
A week over that year.

After awhile
I began hurting too much
And learned that if I devoured
A can of Pringles
Or a half dozen donuts
That I wouldn't think about it anymore
And I wouldn't be as tempted to
Disagree with his absolute authority.

I gained sixty pounds
And he told me that he
Had fallen out of love with me,
But that he could see himself
Loving me again
If I changed
And "stopped gaining
So much fucking weight."

By the time I left him
I was 220 lbs.
I felt swollen, frightened,
Uncomfortably visible
And invisible.

I retreated into
My shelter bedroom
And slept endlessly
While my brain repaired itself
And I was surrounded by people

Who believed that
I actually wasn't
A total piece of shit.

Pupa

Wrapped in a blanket,
Staring at concrete blocks and cracks,
Listening to me.

It rains inside me--
Drips from my amygdala
Flow to memories.

Can't cry- no tears left.
I hear his voice thundering
Inside my head.

My young self whispers,
"I am still here, just buried
Deep in the water."

I wait for it all to drain off.
Sharp pebbles scrape my psyche.

Make It Make Sense

I was told that parking crookedly
Was humiliating to him
And he didn't want his neighbors
To see me with him--

I was told that getting a cold sore
Was a sign that I was cheating on him
And had contracted an STD--

And,
I was told that
Eating carbs and protein
After my blood sugar dropped dangerously low
Spoiled the dinner
That he was going to make
For me, and proved
How horribly inconsiderate
I truly was.

Moving

There is a sign that hangs
Over my TV:
"New Home, New Beginnings,
New Memories."
I took it with me from the
Furniture closet at the shelter
And put it up as the first decoration
In my first apartment.

When I moved into my place
I was afraid of the moving men.
I worried that they would
Tell me that I needed to get rid
Of all my stuff,
Or that they would refuse to help me.

Of course, they were kind--
They put together my dining room table
And chairs,
And one of them picked up my Rainbow Fish
And said it stirred up
Old childhood memories of
The shiny Rainbow Fish book,
The same way it had for me.

Later that night,
I moved my hundred-pound mattress
Into position by myself.
I installed shelves, built storage units
And an entertainment center,
And a few months later began
Planting my flowers.

My home is mine.
I don't have to get rid of
Half of my stuff.
I don't have to only have ten
Or fewer houseplants.
I don't have to worry
About anyone calling me
Materialistic or vain
For having a makeup collection
1/50th the size of most YouTubers'.

And it's been pure bliss.

Mochi

I didn't expect it to be as perfect as it was.
He wasn't my first choice of cat.
His picture didn't instantly excite me.
But he did pick me.

In his first two weeks living with me,
My new Russian Blue cat Mochi
Posted himself as official security cat,
Monitoring the comings and goings of
The residents outside my window,
And once growling slightly
When one got too close.

He also signed up for the job
Of shower monitor,
Peeking in with wide eyes
And meowing in concern,
Asking if he needed to save
Me from drowning in the hot water
Because he would never
Enter it himself.

Several months later,
He is my cuddle buddy
And best friend.

He reminds me gently of when 5 pm
Has arrived by pulling
My hand away from the keyboard
With his soft paw.

He knows that when
My morning alarm goes off,
It's time for me to get up,
And jumps up to give me
Face kisses until I get out of bed.

He keeps me company
When I am cleaning
And watering the plants,
Supervising to make sure that
Everything is going well.

He loves to arrange himself
In "baby position" in my arms,
Opening up his fluffy belly
For me to pet and staring up
At me with his huge green eyes.

I joke that he is my unpaid home health nurse
In addition to my emotional support animal
Because he is constantly aware
Of where I'm at and if I'm safe and doing ok.

I named him Mochi because I love the

Japanese dessert—soft and squishy,
With sweet ice cream on the inside.
Somehow, he always knows how to
Position himself to make me comfortable
And to remind me that
Even if I haven't lost all my extra weight yet,
He still loves me anyway.

Me

Over time, I found myself
Curled into a tiny ball
And poked her outside

To put her feet in
The sunshine-warmed dirt, to watch
The seedlings grow tall.

She looked around, scared
That if she laughed too loudly
He'd come roaring back.

But I promised her
She'd be always protected,
So she ran to play.

Makeover

Piece by piece--
My hair is blonde again;
I wear whatever lipstick shade
I want to again.

I'm not brave enough
To wear a crop top;
I'm still working on my weight.

In two years I plan
To rent a house
With a yard for a small garden
And space for my friends
And I to gather.

I'm diving in
And out of church,
Like the clownfish
In the anemone,
Because I'm still scared,
But I'm trying.

I have an art studio,
A small patio garden,
And a kitchen where I

Can learn to cook.

I have myself.
I wake up each day and
Remind myself--
I am wanted, I am loved,
I am redeemed,
And I will never allow
Anyone to abuse me again.

Some days, it is hard
To fully inhabit myself;
I've learned
That my authentic self
Is like the fairies of Peter Pan:
I have to clap and sing
And tell her how much
I believe in her
For her to come forth
And spread pixie-dust-joy
Over those who welcome her.

Flight

The butterfly spreads
Her wings wide, fanning the sky,
Happily bobbing.

Her cocoon drops down
To the leafy forest floor
Where it lies empty.

She doesn't look back,
But keeps drifting, spinning on
The late summer breeze.

She joins her bright friends
Sipping from yellow flowers
Laughing with wings open.

They don't remember winter;
They live and fly forward.

www.ingramcontent.com/pod-product-compliance
Lightning Source LLC
Chambersburg PA
CBHW051737130826
49812CB00033B/902
9789357211628